JONNY ZUCKER
began his career in radio
and is now a writer and primary school teacher.
Along the way he has played in several bands
and has worked as a stand-up comedian. Jonny has written
two books for adults: *A Class Act* and *Dream Decoder*.
He lives in London with his wife
and their young son.

JAN BARGER'S
previous titles include *Bible Stories for the Very Young*,
Busy Town, and the *Little Animals* series: *Incy Wincy Moo-Cow*,
Who Can Fly?, *Who Eats This?* and
Who Lives Here?

For Jake and Ben – J.Z.

Lighting a Lamp copyright © Frances Lincoln Limited 2004
Text copyright © Jonny Zucker 2004
Illustrations copyright © Jan Barger 2004

First published in Great Britain in 2004 by
Frances Lincoln Children's Books, 4 Torriano Mews,
Torriano Avenue, London NW5 2RZ
www.franceslincoln.com

First paperback edition 2005

British Library Cataloguing in Publication Data available on request

ISBN 978-1-84507-293-3

Printed in Singapore

3 5 7 9 8 6 4 2

The Publishers would like to thank Prodeepta Das for acting as
consultant on this book and for writing the information page.

FESTIVAL TIME!

Lighting a Lamp

A Divali Story

Jonny Zucker

Illustrated by Jan Barger

F

FRANCES LINCOLN
CHILDREN'S BOOKS

It's Divali – the start of the Hindu New Year.
We hear the story about Prince Rama
fighting the demon Ravana to
rescue his wife, Sita.

We put special rangoli patterns
on our doorstep, so that
the goddess Lakshmi will bring us
good luck in the year ahead.

I make delicious coconut barfi
in the kitchen, to enjoy the sweetness
of the Divali celebration.

We go to the temple to offer prayers and sweets to Rama and Sita.

I exchange gifts and sweets
with all of my friends and cousins.
We look forward to good things
in our New Year.

We light small lamps called divas,
just as people did to welcome home
Rama, Sita and Lakshman.

At night there is a brilliant
firework display to celebrate
Divali - our festival of lights.

What is Divali about?

Divali, or Deepavali, means a row of lamps (**divas**). It is one of the most important festivals for Hindus everywhere. It reminds people of celebrations to welcome the return of Rama after fourteen years of exile. It also marks the end of one year and the beginning of another.

According to the Ramayana, one of the two Indian epics, when Rama was about to be crowned, his father banished him in order to honour an oath to his stepmother, who wanted her own son to be king. Rama's wife, Sita and his brother, Lakshman followed him into the forest. Life in the forest was full of trials and tribulations. Sita was abducted by the demon king, Ravana, and was taken to the island of Lanka. Hanuman, the leader of the monkeys and totally devoted to Rama, played a major role in rescuing Sita. After fourteen years, Rama returned with his wife and brother to a hero's welcome and took his rightful place as the king. Rama was a very good king, who always put the interests of his subjects first and foremost, and he was widely loved and respected. In fact, Rama is believed by Hindus to be an incarnation of God.

In India, Divali is celebrated differently in different parts. In Gujurat, Maharashtra and West Bengal, it involves worship of **Lakshmi**, the goddess of wealth. Houses are decorated with **rangoli** (colourful rice powder) patterns including motifs of (Lakshmi's) feet and lotus flowers. Divali is an occasion for enjoyment. People wear new clothes and give sweets to one another. Verandahs are lit up with twinkling, little earthern lamps – called divas – and noisy fireworks fill the night sky.

More titles in the *Festival Time!* series by Jonny Zucker

Lanterns and Firecrackers – A Chinese New Year Story

Follow a family as they let off firecrackers,
watch lion and dragon dances and hang up lanterns
to celebrate the start of their New Year.

ISBN 1-84507-076-3

Sweet Dates to Eat – A Ramadan and Eid Story

Follow a family as they fast each day,
go to the mosque on the Night of Power,
and enjoy a delicious feast.

ISBN 1-84507-294-4

Hope and New Life! – An Easter Story

Follow a family as they take Holy Communion,
eat hot cross buns, go on an Easter egg hunt
and watch a big parade.

ISBN 1-84507-274-X

Frances Lincoln titles are available from all good bookshops.
You can also buy books and find out more about your favourite titles,
authors and illustrators on our website: www.franceslincoln.com